WORLD OF WONDER

AMAZING ANIMAL BABIES

Written by Kay Barnham

Illustrated by Maddie Frost

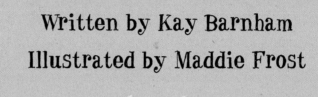

CRABTREE
PUBLISHING COMPANY
WWW.CRABTREEBOOKS.COM

CRABTREE
PUBLISHING COMPANY
WWW.CRABTREEBOOKS.COM

Words with lines underneath, like this, can be found in the glossary on page 32.

Author: Kay Barnham

Editorial Director: Kathy Middleton

Editors: Victoria Brooker, Janine Deschenes

Proofreader: Melissa Boyce

Creative director: Paul Cherrill

Illustrator: Maddie Frost

**Production coordinator and
 Prepress technician:** Tammy McGarr

Print coordinator: Katherine Berti

Library and Achives Canada Cataloguing in Publication

Title: Amazing animal babies / written by Kay Barnham ;
 illustrated by Maddie Frost.
Names: Barnham, Kay, author. | Frost, Maddie, illustrator.
Description: Series statement: World of wonder |
 Originally published: London: Wayland, 2018. |
 Includes bibliographical references and index.
Identifiers: Canadiana (print) 20200220330 | Canadiana (ebook) 20200220349
 ISBN 9780778782476 (hardcover) |
 ISBN 9780778782513 (softcover) |
 ISBN 9781427126207 (HTML)
Subjects: LCSH: Animals—Infancy—Juvenile literature. |
 LCSH: Parental behavior in animals—Juvenile literature.
Classification: LCC QL763 .B37 2021 | DDC j591.3/92—dc23

Library of Congress Cataloging-in-Publication Data

Names: Barnham, Kay, author. | Frost, Maddie, illustrator.
Title: Amazing animal babies / written by Kay Barnham ;
 illustrated by Maddie Frost.
Description: New York : Crabtree Publishing Company, 2021. |
 Series: World of wonder | First published in 2018 by Wayland.
Identifiers: LCCN 2020015590 (print) | LCCN 2020015591 (ebook) |
 ISBN 9780778782476 (hardcover) | ISBN 9780778782513 (paperback) |
 ISBN 9781427126207 (ebook)
Subjects: LCSH: Animals--Infancy--Juvenile literature.
Classification: LCC QL763 .B36 2021 (print) | LCC QL763 (ebook) |
 DDC 591.3/92--dc23
LC record available at https://lccn.loc.gov/2020015590
LC ebook record available at https://lccn.loc.gov/2020015591

Crabtree Publishing Company

www.crabtreebooks.com   1-800-387-7650
Published by Crabtree Publishing Company in 2021

First published in 2018 by Wayland
Copyright ©Hodder and Stoughton 2018

Printed in the U.S.A./072020/CG20200429

Published in Canada
Crabtree Publishing
616 Welland Avenue
St. Catharines, Ontario
L2M 5V6

Published in the United States
Crabtree Publishing
347 Fifth Ave
Suite 1402-145
New York, NY 10016

NOTES FOR PARENTS AND TEACHERS

This series encourages children to observe the wonderful world around them. Here are some ideas to help children get more out of this book.

1. Ask children to make a list of animal babies. Next, create a T-Chart. On one side, list the animal babies that look like their parents. On the other side, list the animal babies that do not look like their parents. Use a T-Chart to compare animal babies in other ways too.

2. Visit a farm in springtime or watch a live feed from a zoo. Which baby animals can the children see? Have them draw a picture of the baby animal. Then, have them predict what the animal will look like in one year. Have them draw a picture to show how the animal will change.

3. Suggest that the children paint a picture of the farm or zoo and include all the animal babies that they saw there (see number 2).

4. Have children match the name of an animal with the name of its baby. For example: kangaroo and joey; bear and cub; sheep and lamb.

5. If you have a puppy, kitten, bunny, or other baby pet—or you know someone who does—take a photo of it every week so that children can see how it grows into an adult.

Did you know that there are millions
of different kinds of animals?
All kinds of animals have babies.

Animal babies depend on their parents for food and safety. They need to grow and learn the skills they need to <u>survive</u>.

Some animals have live babies. Most of these animals are called <u>mammals</u>. Live young come from their mothers' bodies. They breathe right away. A tall giraffe gives birth standing up. The baby falls toward the ground head first! This <u>shocks</u> the baby into taking its first breath.

6

A baby zebra can stand
after only a few minutes.
This is important because
it needs to be able to
run from <u>predators</u>!

Other animals, such as birds and most <u>reptiles</u>, lay eggs. The baby animal inside the egg keeps growing until it is ready to <u>hatch</u>. A male emperor penguin keeps an egg warm for weeks until it hatches.

Birds, frogs, turtles, crocodiles, and most fish and snakes lay eggs. Millions of years ago, dinosaurs laid eggs too!

Some animal babies look like their
parents. They are just much smaller.
Tiger babies, called cubs,
have the same orange fur
and dark stripes as their parents.

10

Snow leopard cubs have the same
markings as adult snow leopards.
They are also born with the same
thick coats and large paws.

Some animal babies look very different from their parents. A baby frog is called a tadpole. It has a long, wiggly tail. But as weeks pass, it grows four legs. Its tail shrinks and goes away. Now it's a frog that looks like its parents!

A baby swan is called a cygnet.
These cygnets have brown, fluffy feathers.
But they will become long-necked swans.
They will grow feathers like their parents.

Some animal babies need a lot of care.
A baby koala is called a joey. When it is born,
a joey cannot see or hear. It crawls into its
mother's <u>pouch</u> and stays there for about six months.
Even when it leaves the pouch, the joey stays with
its mother until it's around one year old.

Baby kangaroos are called joeys too.
They also grow inside their mothers' pouches.
Newborns are as small as jelly beans!

15

A few animal babies do not need
care from their parents.
They are ready to survive on their
own from the very beginning.
Baby sea turtles hatch alone.
Then they run to the ocean.

Some snakes give birth to live young.
Others lay eggs. But almost all snakes
leave their babies to look after themselves.

Animal babies need food to grow bigger and stronger.
Bats feed their babies milk for a few weeks.
Then the babies learn to find their own food.
Some eat insects. Others eat fruit.

A baby orangutan drinks its mother's milk for years. Sometimes, it drinks its mother's milk until it is more than eight years old! Adult orangutans mostly eat fruit.

Some animals need fat
on their bodies to keep them warm.
Animal babies must grow the body fat they need.
Seals do not have enough body fat as babies.
They huddle together to stay warm
while their mothers find food.

Ocean waters can be very, very cold.
A sea otter carries her pup
on her chest for two months.
This keeps the pup cozy and warm.

Animals keep their babies safe from predators.
Sometimes, adult elephants form
a circle around their babies, called calves.
The circle guards the calves from lions and hyenas.

An antelope keeps her baby
hidden during the day
while she searches for food.

23

Many animal babies learn by playing.
Wolf babies are called pups.
They fight with each other just for fun.
But they also are learning fighting skills
that they'll need as they get older.

A bear fight can be very noisy.
But when bear cubs play-fight,
they are quiet and their bites are gentle.

Some animals have a lot of babies at once.
A rabbit can have a <u>litter</u> of as many as 14 babies!

Other animals have just
one baby to look after.
A horse usually has
one baby at a time.
A baby horse is called a foal.

When the animals grow up,
they will have babies of their own.
Then there will be more animal babies to care for!

This cheetah is looking after
her new babies, called cubs.
What's your favorite animal baby?

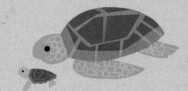

THINGS TO DO

1. Make a mask of the face of your favorite animal baby! Decorate a paper plate with paint, cotton balls, yarn, or anything that you can find to make the animal baby's face look just like the real thing.

2. Draw, paint a picture, or cut out pictures to make a collage of your favorite animal baby.

3. Create a word cloud of animal babies! Add the names of all the different animal babies you can think of. Write them all down using different-colored pens. Start like this...

CUB JOEY PUPPY

LEARNING MORE

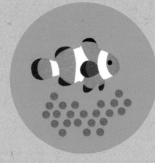

Books

Barwick, Laura. *Animal Babies*. BBC Books, 2016.

Kalman, Bobbie. *How Do Baby Animals Learn*? Crabtree Publishing, 2012.

Kalman, Bobbie. *Wolf Family Adventures.* Crabtree Publishing, 2016.

Websites

Learn all about a variety of animal species.
www.kids.nationalgeographic. com/animals/

See pictures and videos of the newest baby animals at zoos and aquariums around the world.
www.zooborns.com

GLOSSARY

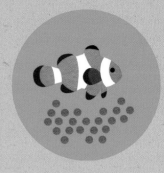

hatch To come out of an egg

litter A group of baby animals born at the same time

mammals Animals that are warm-blooded and feed their young with milk. Most mammals have live young.

markings Patterns on an animal's body

pouch A pocket of skin on the stomachs of some animals that is used to carry babies

predators Animals that hunt and eat other animals

reptiles Animals, such as snakes and lizards, that are cold-blooded and have scales. Most reptiles lay eggs.

shocks Surprises suddenly

survive To stay alive